HAL•LEONARD

ESSENTIAL SONGS

PIANO VOCAL GUITAR

The 1960s

ISBN 0-634-09103-4

HAL•LEONARD®
CORPORATION

7777 W. BLUEMOUND RD. P.O. BOX 13819 MILWAUKEE, WI 53213

Visit Hal Leonard Online at
www.halleonard.com

CONTENTS

199	Johnny Angel	Shelley Fabares	1	1962
202	Lady Madonna	The Beatles	4	1968
206	Last Date	Floyd Cramer	2	1960
209	Let's Hang On	The 4 Seasons	3	1965
214	A Little Bit Me, A Little Bit You	The Monkees	2	1967
220	The Loco-Motion	Little Eva	1	1962
217	Love Is Blue (L'amour Est Bleu)	Paul Mauriat	1	1968
224	MacArthur Park	Richard Harris	2	1968
236	Midnight Confessions	The Grass Roots	5	1968
239	Mrs. Brown You've Got a Lovely Daughter	Herman's Hermits	1	1965
242	My Guy	Mary Wells	1	1964
247	Never My Love	The Association	2	1967
250	1 2 3	Len Barry	2	1965
253	Our Day Will Come	Ruby & The Romantics	1	1963
256	People Got to Be Free	The Rascals	1	1968
260	Pleasant Valley Sunday	The Monkees	3	1967
272	Please Love Me Forever	Bobby Vinton	6	1967
274	Please Mr. Postman	The Marvelettes	1	1961
280	Ramblin' Rose	Nat King Cole	2	1962
267	Respect	Aretha Franklin	1	1967
282	Ruby Baby	Dion	2	1963
290	Ruby, Don't Take Your Love to Town	Kenny Rogers	6	1969
294	Save the Last Dance for Me	The Drifters	1	1960
285	Sherry	The 4 Seasons	1	1962
298	The Shoop Shoop Song (It's in His Kiss)	Betty Everett	6	1964
304	Shop Around	The Miracles	2	1961
301	Sloop John B	The Beach Boys	3	1966
308	Soldier Boy	The Shirelles	1	1962
310	Something	The Beatles	3	1966
313	Spooky	Classics IV	3	1968
318	Stand by Me	Ben E. King	4	1961
326	Stay	Maurice Williams & The Zodiacs	1	1960
321	Stop! In the Name of Love	The Supremes	1	1965
328	Summer in the City	The Lovin' Spoonful	1	1966
331	Surf City	Jan & Dean	1	1963
334	Suspicious Minds	Elvis Presley	1	1969
340	Sweet Caroline	Neil Diamond	4	1969
346	There's a Kind of Hush (All Over the World)	Herman's Hermits	4	1967
350	A Time for Us (Love Theme)	Henry Mancini	1	1969
356	Town Without Pity	Jean Pitney	13	1962
353	Traces	Classics IV	2	1969
360	Travelin' Man	Ricky Nelson	1	1961
366	Twist and Shout	The Beatles/The Isley Brothers	2/17	1964/62
363	Under the Boardwalk	The Drifters	4	1964
370	Wedding Bell Blues	The 5th Dimension	1	1969
374	Where the Boys Are	Connie Francis	4	1961
382	White Rabbit	Jefferson Airplane	8	1967
377	Will You Love Me Tomorrow (Will You Still Love Me Tomorrow)	The Shirelles	1	1961
386	Windy	The Association	1	1967
389	World Without Love	Peter and Gordon	1	1964
398	Yesterday	The Beatles	1	1965
392	You Keep Me Hangin' On	The Supremes/Vanilla Fudge	1/6	1966/68

AND WHEN I DIE

Words and Music by
LAURA NYRO

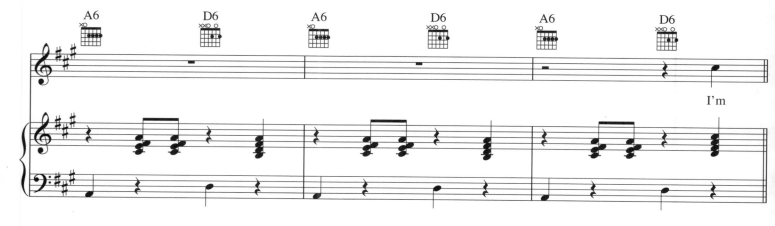

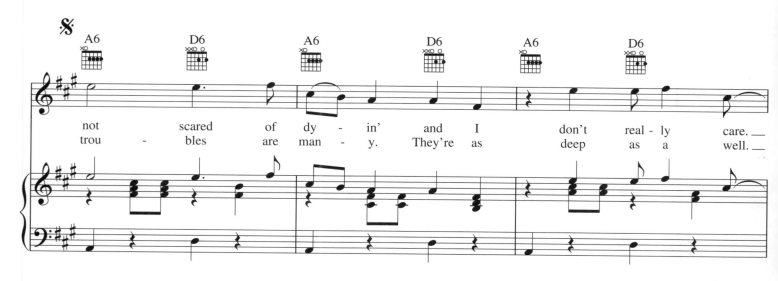

not — scared of dy - in' and I don't real - ly care. __
trou - bles are man - y. They're as deep as a well. __

BABY I NEED YOUR LOVIN'

Words and Music by BRIAN HOLLAND,
LAMONT DOZIER and EDWARD HOLLAND

beg. _____ Then weak I'd _____ rath-er be,_____ If it means hav-

ing you to keep, _____ "Cause late - ly I've been los-ing sleep. _____

Chorus:

Ba - by, I need _____ your lov - in'; Got _____ to have all _____ your lov - in'.

Ba -- by I need _____ your lov - in'; Got _____ to have all _____ your lov - in'.

Lonely nights —— echo your name, ——————— Oh, —— some-times I

won-der —— will I ev-er be the same? ——— Oh yeah!

When you see me smil-ing, you know —— things ——————— have got-ten worse. ——

An-y smile — you might see —— has all ——— been re-hearsed. ——

Dar-ling, I —— can't go on with-out you. This emp-ti-ness won't let me live with-out you;

This lone-li-ness in - side me, dar-ling, makes — me feel half a - live. —

Chorus:
Ba - by, I need —— your lov-in'; —— got —— to have all —— your lov - in';

repeat and fade

Ba - by, I need —— your lov - in'; got —— to have all —— your lov - in'.

BABY LOVE

Words and Music by BRIAN HOLLAND,
EDWARD HOLLAND and LAMONT DOZIER

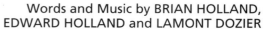

Ba - by love, my ba - by love, I
Ba - by love, my ba - by love, why
me, my love, my ba - by love, I

need you oh how I need __ you.
must we sep - a - rate my love?
need ya, oh how I need __ ya.

But all you do is
All of my
Why you do me

treat me bad, _____ break my heart and leave me sad. _____
whole life through, ____ I nev - er love no one but you. _____
like you do, _____ af - ter I've been true to you. _____

BIG GIRLS DON'T CRY

Words and Music by BOB CREWE
and BOB GAUDIO

BARBARA ANN

Words and Music by
FRED FASSERT

(Ba, ba, ba, ba, ___ Ba' - 'bra Ann. Ba, ba, ba, ba, ___ Ba' - 'bra Ann)

Ba' - 'bra

Ann, _____ take ___ my hand. _____ Ba' - 'bra

Ann, _____ you got me rock-in' and a-roll-in', rock-

25

BECAUSE THEY'RE YOUNG

Lyric by AARON SCHROEDER and WALLY GOLD
Music by DON COSTA

BORN TO BE WILD

Words and Music by
MARS BONFIRE

(1., 3.) Get your mo-tor run - ning. _____ Head out on the high - way _____
(2.) I like smoke and light - ning, _____ heav - y met - al thun - der _____

look - ing for ad - ven - ture in what -
rac - ing in the wind _____ and the

ev - er comes our way. _____ Yeah, dar - ling, gon - na
feel - ing that I'm un - der _____

Born to be wild. _____

COME BACK WHEN YOU GROW UP

Words and Music by
MARTHA SHARP

BREAKING UP IS HARD TO DO

Words and Music by HOWARD GREENFIELD
and NEIL SEDAKA

BROWN EYED GIRL

Words and Music by
VAN MORRISON

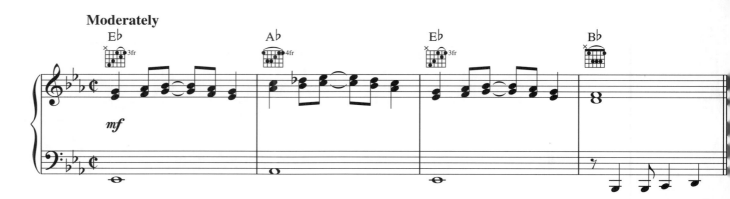

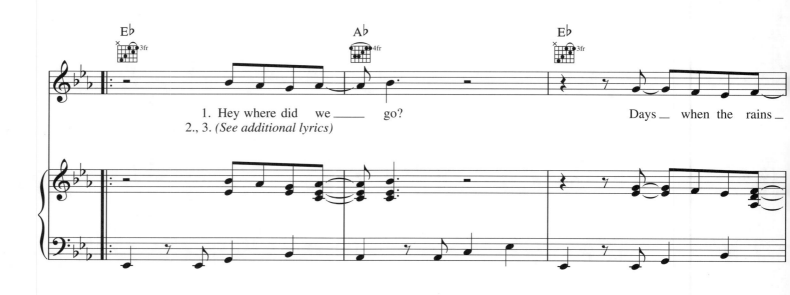

1. Hey where did we ___ go?
2., 3. (See additional lyrics)

Days ___ when the rains ___

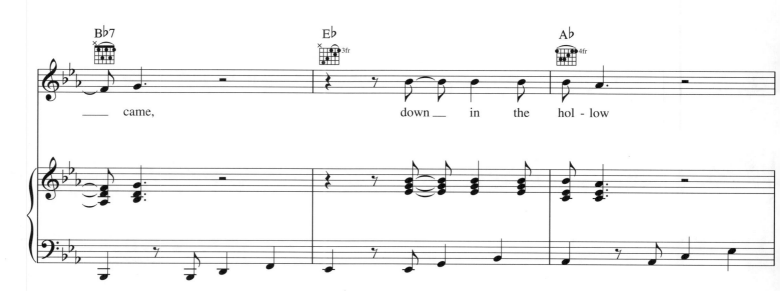

___ came,

down ___ in the hol - low

Additional Lyrics

2. Whatever happened to Tuesday and so slow
   Going down the old mine with a transistor radio
   Standing in the sunlight laughing
   Hiding behind a rainbow's wall
   Slipping and a-sliding
   All along the water fall
   With you, my brown eyed girl
   You, my brown eyed girl.
   Do you remember when we used to sing:
   Chorus

3. So hard to find my way, now that I'm all on my own
   I saw you just the other day, my, how you have grown
   Cast my memory back there, Lord
   Sometime I'm overcome thinking 'bout
   Making love in the green grass
   Behind the stadium
   With you, my brown eyed girl
   With you, my brown eyed girl.
   Do you remember when we used to sing:
   Chorus

CALIFORNIA GIRLS

Words and Music by BRIAN WILSON
and MIKE LOVE

*Recorded one half step higher.

CAN'T BUY ME LOVE

Words and Music by JOHN LENNON
and PAUL McCARTNEY

CAN'T HELP FALLING IN LOVE

Words and Music by GEORGE DAVID WEISS,
HUGO PERETTI and LUIGI CREATORE

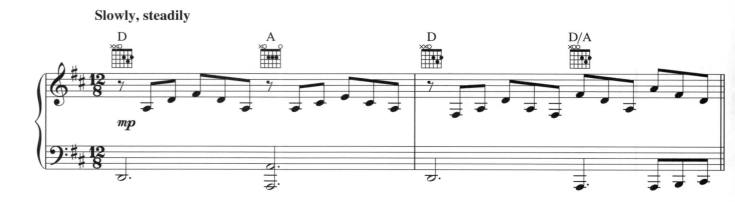

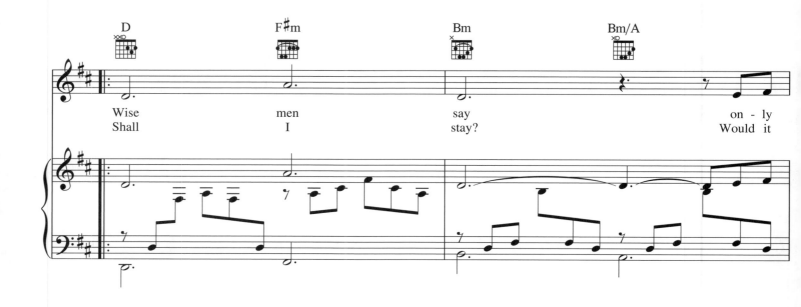

Wise men say only
Shall I stay?

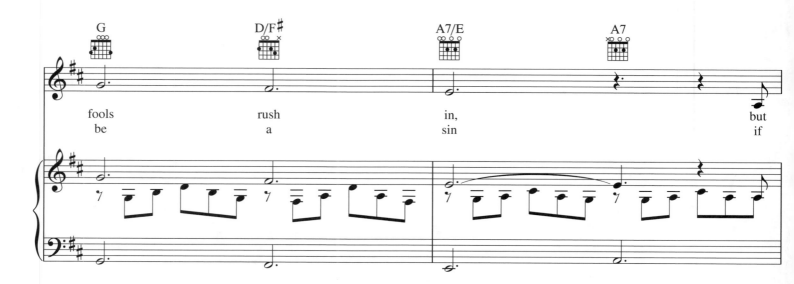

fools rush in, but
be a sin if

CAN'T TAKE MY EYES OFF OF YOU

Words and Music by BOB CREWE
and BOB GAUDIO

You're just too

good to be true, ___ can't take my eyes off of you. ___ You'd be like
way that I stare, ___ there's noth-ing else to com-pare. ___ The sight of

heav-en to touch, I wan-na hold you so much. At long last
you leaves me weak, there are no words left to speak. But if you

CRYING IN THE CHAPEL

Words and Music by
ARTIE GLENN

Slowly, with expression

Chorus

F

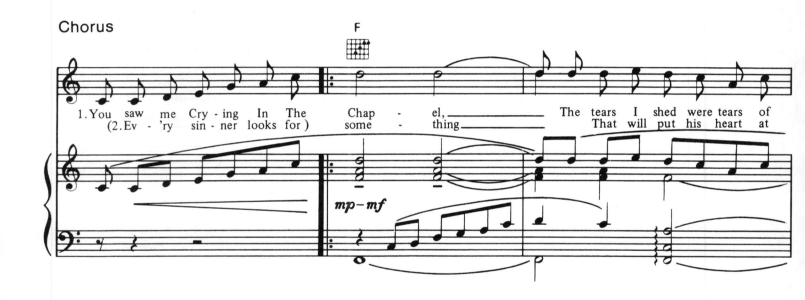

1. You saw me Cry-ing In The Chap- el,_____ The tears I shed were tears of
(2. Ev- 'ry sin- ner looks for) some- thing_____ That will put his heart at

C   A7   D7   Fm6

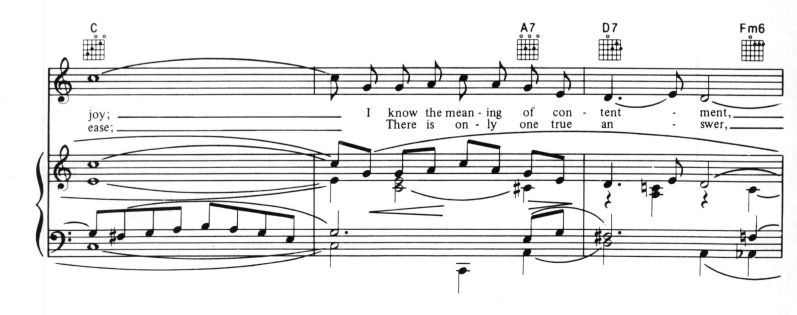

joy;_____ I know the mean- ing of con- tent- ment,_____
ease;_____ There is on- ly one true an- swer,_____

CRYSTAL BLUE PERSUASION

Words and Music by TOMMY JAMES,
ED GRAY and MIKE VALE

With a Rock beat

Look o-ver yon - der, what do you see?___
gon-na see the ___ light.___

The sun is a-ris - in'
Love, love is the an - swer,

most def-i-nite-ly. ___
that's all right. ___

A new day's com -
So don't you give up ___

DANCING IN THE STREET

Words and Music by MARVIN GAYE,
IVY HUNTER and WILLIAM STEVENSON

Moderately, with a steady beat

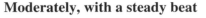

Call - ing out __ a - round __ the world, are you
in - vi - ta - tion a - cross the na - tion, a

read - y for a brand-new beat? __ Sum - mer's here __ and the
chance for folks to meet. __ There'll be laugh - ing, sing - ing __ and

time is right __ for danc - ing in the street. __ They're danc - ing in Chi -
mu - sic swing - ing, danc - ing in the street. __ Phil - a - del - phia, P. A.,

DAYDREAM BELIEVER

Words and Music by
JOHN STEWART

DID YOU EVER HAVE TO MAKE UP YOUR MIND?

Words and Music by
JOHN SEBASTIAN

DEDICATED TO THE ONE I LOVE

Words and Music by LOWMAN PAULING
and RALPH BASS

Moderately

D.S. al Coda I

DO YOU KNOW THE WAY TO SAN JOSE

Lyric by HAL DAVID
Music by BURT BACHARACH

Moderately, rhythmically

Do you know the way to San __ Jo - se? I've been a - way so
You can real - ly breathe in San __ Jo - se. They've got a lot of

DON'T LET THE SUN CATCH YOU CRYING

Words and Music by GERARD MARSDEN, FRED MARSDEN,
LES CHADWICK and LES MAGUIRE

DOWNTOWN

Words and Music by
TONY HATCH

THE END OF THE WORLD

Words by SYLVIA DEE
Music by ARTHUR KENT

Melancholy Ballad

Why does the sun go on shin - ing?

Why does the sea rush to shore?

Don't they know it's the end of the world, 'cause

ELI'S COMIN'

Words and Music by
LAURA NYRO

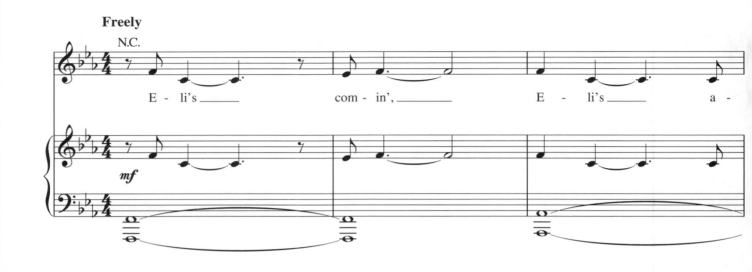

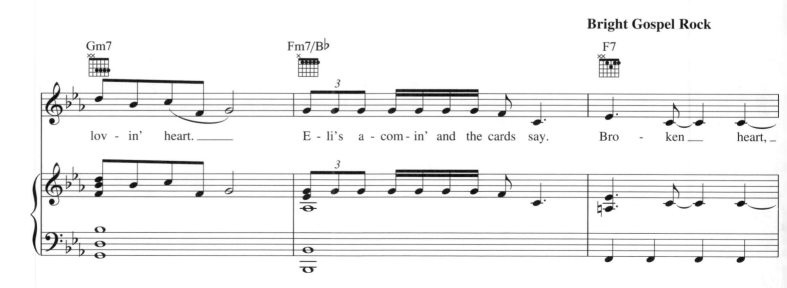

FOR ONCE IN MY LIFE

Words by RONALD MILLER
Music by ORLANDO MURDEN

GET BACK

Words and Music by JOHN LENNON
and PAUL McCARTNEY

Moderately

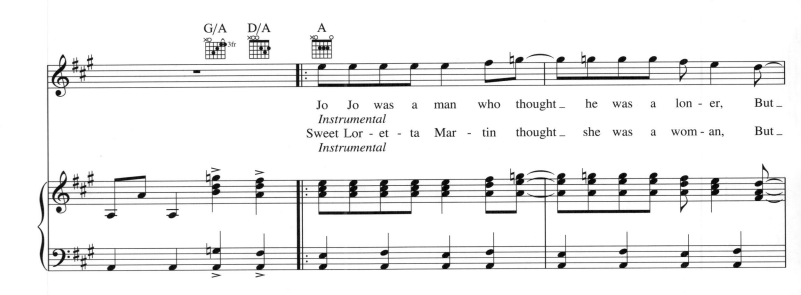

Jo Jo was a man who thought ___ he was a lon - er, But ___
Instrumental
Sweet Lor - et - ta Mar - tin thought ___ she was a wom - an, But ___
Instrumental

___ he knew it could - n't last. ___   Jo ___ Jo left his home in Tuc -
___ she was an - oth - er man. ___   All ___ the girls a - round her say ___

GOIN' OUT OF MY HEAD

Words and Music by TEDDY RANDAZZO
and BOBBY WEINSTEIN

want you to want me | I need you so bad-ly, I
see you each morn-ing; but you just walk past me, you

can't think of an-y-thing but you. ___ And I
don't e-ven know that I ex-

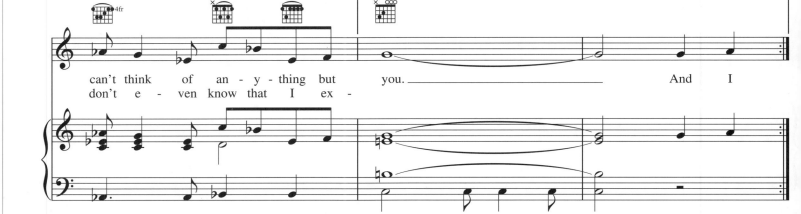

ist. ___ Go-'in out of my head ___ o-ver you, _ out of my

head ___ o-ver you. _ Out of my head day ___ and night,

GIMME SOME LOVIN'

Words and Music by STEVE WINWOOD,
MUFF WINWOOD and SPENCER DAVIS

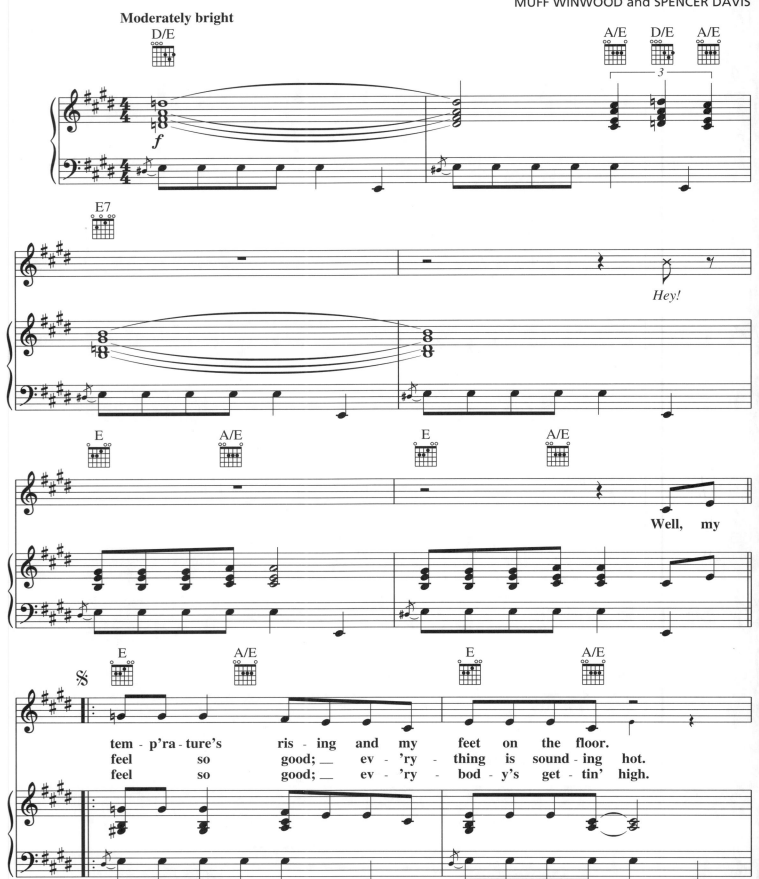

Hey!

Well, my

tem - p'ra - ture's ris - ing and my feet on the floor.
feel so good; __ ev - 'ry - thing is sound - ing hot.
feel so good; __ ev - 'ry - bod - y's get - tin' high.

GOOD LOVIN'

Words and Music by RUDY CLARK
and ARTHUR RESNICK

GOOD VIBRATIONS

Words and Music by BRIAN WILSON
and MIKE LOVE

GREENBACK DOLLAR

Words and Music by HOYT AXTON
and KEN RAMSEY

can. For a wail-in' song _ and a good gui - tar, _ the on - ly things that I un - der - stand, _

_ poh boy, _ the on - ly things that I un - der - stand. _____

The on - ly things that I un - der - stand, ___ poh boy, ___ the

on - ly things that I un - der - stand. _____

A GROOVY KIND OF LOVE

Words and Music by TONI WINE
and CAROLE BAYER SAGER

Slowly

When I'm feel-in' blue, all I have to do is take a look at
want to, you can turn me on to an-y-thing you

you, then I'm not so _____ blue. When you're close to me, I can feel your
want to, an-y-time at _____ all. When I kiss your lips, oo, I start to

heart beat, I can hear you breath-ing _____ in _____ my _____ ear. } Would-n't you a-
shiv-er, can't con-trol the quiv-er-ing _____ in-side.

gree, ba-by, you and me got a groo-vy kind of love.

An-y time you love.

Oh. ___

HANG ON SLOOPY

Words and Music by WES FARRELL
and BERT RUSSELL

HANKY PANKY

Words and Music by JEFF BARRY
and ELLIE GREENWICH

Moderate boogie-Rock

HEATWAVE
(Love Is Like a Heatwave)

Words and Music by EDWARD HOLLAND,
LAMONT DOZIER and BRIAN HOLLAND

HELP ME RHONDA

Words and Music by BRIAN WILSON
and MIKE LOVE

I CAN'T STOP LOVING YOU

Words and Music by
DON GIBSON

HEY JUDE

Words and Music by JOHN LENNON
and PAUL McCARTNEY

HEY PAULA

Words and Music by
RAY HILDEBRAND

I GOT YOU
(I Feel Good)

Words and Music by
JAMES BROWN

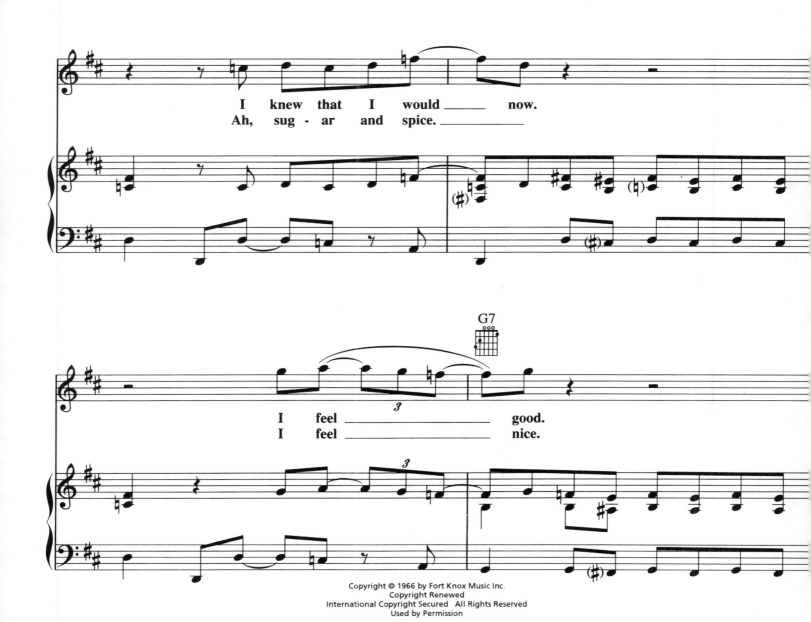

I'M HENRY VIII, I AM

Words and Music by FRED MURRAY
and R.P. WESTON

With a bright steady beat

I'm Hen-er-y the Eighth, I am!
Hen-er-y the Eighth, I am, I am! ___ I got mar-ried to the
wid-ow next door. She's been mar-ried sev-en times be-fore and

I HEARD IT
THROUGH THE GRAPEVINE

Words and Music by NORMAN J. WHITFIELD
and BARRETT STRONG

Moderately

Mm. _____ I bet you're won-derin' how I knew
_____ ain't sup-posed to cry,
_____ of what you see,

'bout your plans _____ to make me blue, _____ with some oth - er guy.
but these tears _____ I can't hold in - side. _____ Los - in' you
son, and none _____ of what you hear. _____ But I can't help

A7 Em

_____ it through the grape - vine.   Oh, _____   I'm just
_____ it through the grape - vine.   And I'm   just
_____ it through the grape - vine.   Oh, _____   I'm just

A7

a - bout to lose _____ my mind. __ }   Hon - ey, hon - ey, oh
a - bout to lose _____ my mind. __
a - bout to lose _____ my mind. __   (I

Em

yeah.
heard it through the grape - vine, not much long - er would you be mine, ba -

To Coda

1   2

(Ooh. _____   I know a man __
(Ooh. _____   Ooh. _____
- by.) (Yeah, __

I STARTED A JOKE

Words and Music by ROBIN GIBB,
MAURICE GIBB and BARRY GIBB

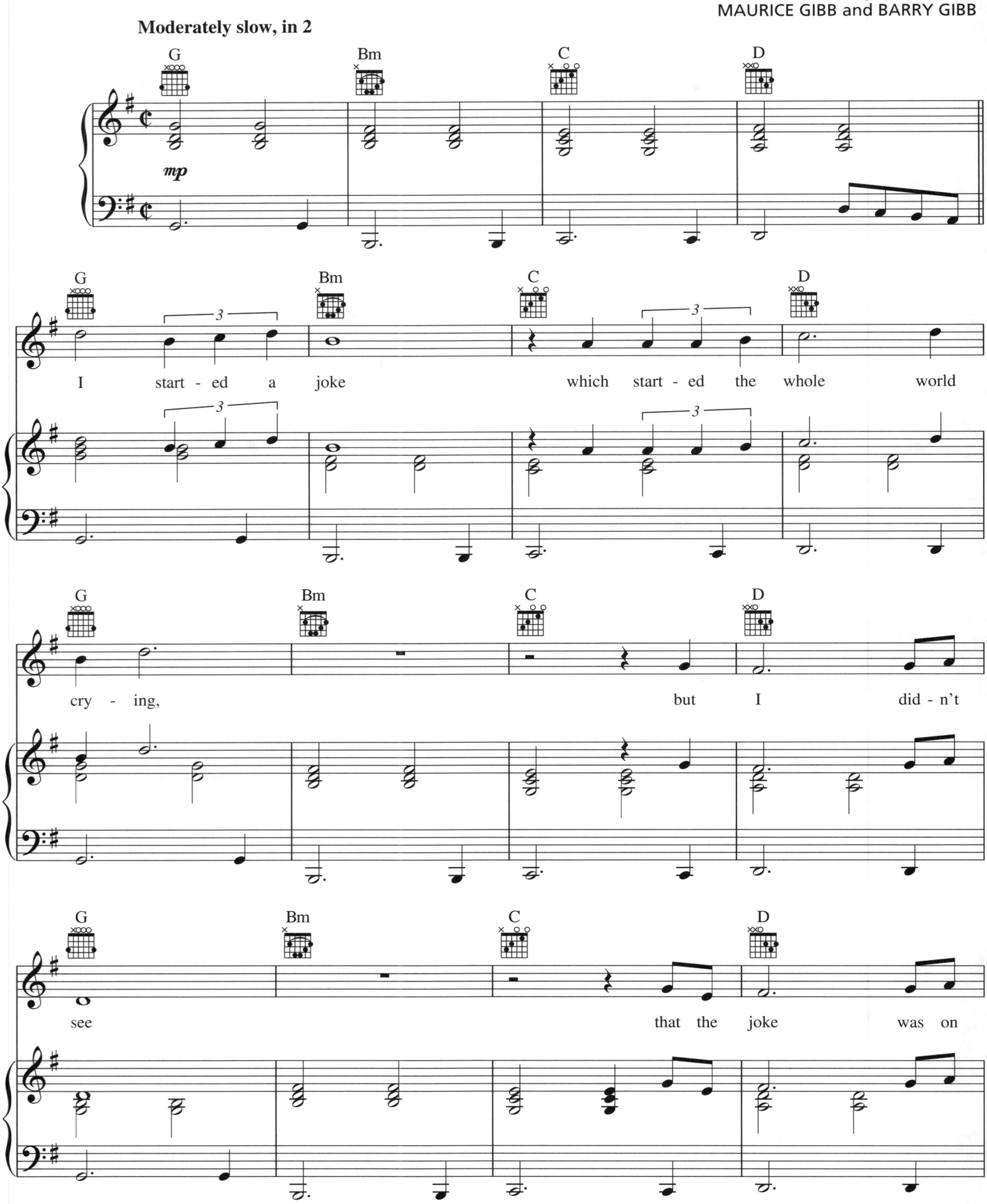

Moderately slow, in 2

I start-ed a joke which start-ed the whole world

cry-ing, but I did-n't

see that the joke was on

I WANT TO HOLD YOUR HAND

Words and Music by JOHN LENNON
and PAUL McCARTNEY

IF I HAD A HAMMER
(The Hammer Song)

Words and Music by LEE HAYS
and PETE SEEGER

INCENSE AND PEPPERMINTS

Words and Music by JOHN CARTER
and TIM GILBERT

yard - stick for lu - na - tics, one point of view. Who cares what

games we choose, Lit - tle to win, but noth - in' to lose.

D.S. al Coda

CODA

in - cense, pep - per - mints, in - cense,

IT'S NOT UNUSUAL

Words and Music by GORDON MILLS
and LES REED

It's not un-u - su-al ___ to be loved by an-y-one. ___
It's not un-u - su-al ___ to go out at an-y-time, ___

It's not un-u - su-al ___ to have
but when I see ___ you out ___ and a-

fun with an-y-one. _____ But when I see ___
bout it's such a crime. _____ If you should ev-

IT HURTS TO BE IN LOVE

Words and Music by HELEN MILLER
and HOWARD GREENFIELD

Additional Lyrics

3. How long can I exist
   Wanting lips I've never kissed
   You give all your kisses to everybody else.

4. You think I'm just a friend.
   Though it hurts I must pretend.
   The only way to keep you, is keep you to myself.

IT MUST BE HIM
(Seul Sur Son Etoile)

Words and Music by GILBERT BECAUD
and MAURICE VIDALIN
English Adaptation by MACK DAVID

IT'S NOW OR NEVER

Words and Music by AARON SCHROEDER
and WALLY GOLD

JIMMY MACK

Words and Music by BRIAN HOLLAND,
LAMONT DOZIER and EDWARD HOLLAND

My arms ___ are miss-ing you, ___ my lips ___ feel the same way too. ___ I tried ___ so hard to be true ___ like ___ I prom-ised to do; ___ but this boy ___ keeps

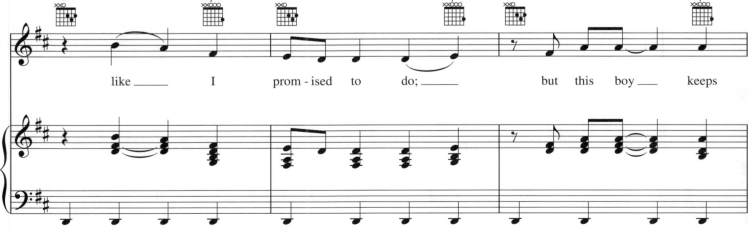

Additional Lyrics

2. He calls me on the phone about three times a day
Now my heart's just listening to what he has to say.
But this loneliness I have within
Keeps reaching out to be his friend.
Hey, Jimmy, Jimmy oh Jimmy Mack,
When are you coming back?
Jimmy, Jimmy oh Jimmy Mack, you better hurry back.

JOHNNY ANGEL

Words by LYNN DUDDY
Music by LEE POCKRISS

LADY MADONNA

Words and Music by JOHN LENNON
and PAUL McCARTNEY

Brightly, with a beat

Lady Madonna, children at your feet, ___
Lady Madonna, baby at your breast, ___
Lady Madonna, lying on the bed, ___
Lady Madonna, children at your feet, ___

Wonder how you manage to make ___
Wonders how you manage to feed ___
Listen to the music playing
Wonder how you manage to make ___

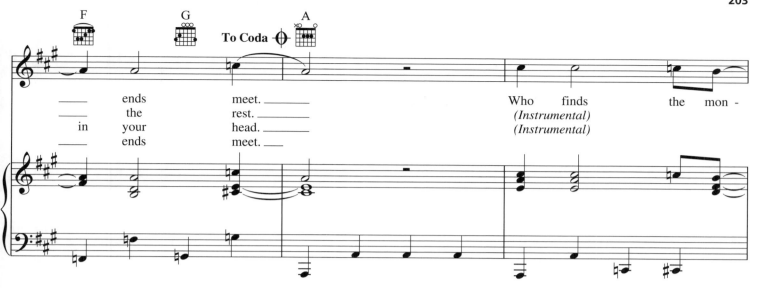

ends _____ meet. _____
the _____ rest. _____
in your _____ head. _____
ends _____ meet. ___

Who finds the mon-
(Instrumental)
(Instrumental)

-ey when you pay the rent? ___

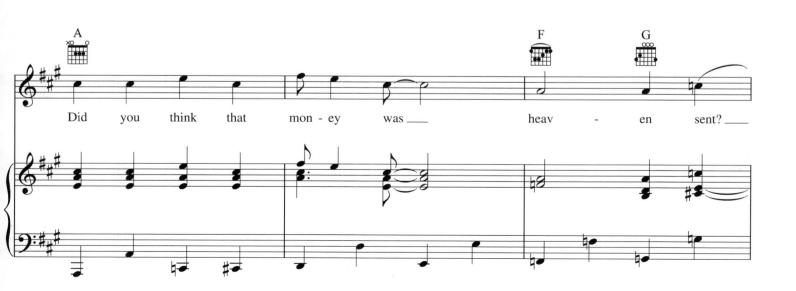

Did you think that mon-ey was ___ heav-en sent? ___

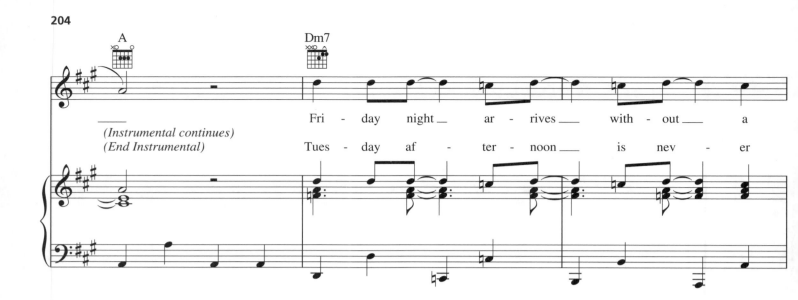

(Instrumental continues)
(End Instrumental)

Fri - day night __ ar - rives __ with - out __ a
Tues - day af - ter - noon __ is nev - er

suit - case, _____
end - ing, _____

Sun - day morn - ing,
Wednes - day morn - ing,

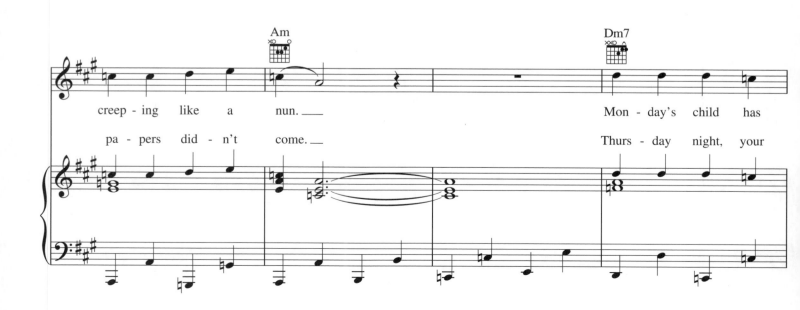

creep - ing like a nun. __
pa - pers did - n't come. __

Mon - day's child has
Thurs - day night, your

LAST DATE

Words and Music by
FLOYD CRAMER

LET'S HANG ON

Words and Music by BOB CREWE,
DENNY RANDELL and SANDY LINZER

Additional Lyrics

2. There isn't anything I wouldn't do.
   I'd pay any price to get in good with you.
   Patch it up. (Give me a second turnin'.)
   Patch it up. (Don't cool off while I'm burnin'.)

   You've got me cryin', dyin' at your door.
   Don't shut me out, ooh, let me in once more.
   Open up. (Your arms, I need to hold you.)
   Open up. (Your heart, oh girl, I love you.)

   Baby, don't you know?
   Baby, don't you go.
   Think it over and stay.

A LITTLE BIT ME, A LITTLE BIT YOU

Words and Music by
NEIL DIAMOND

LOVE IS BLUE
(L'amour Est Bleu)

English Lyric by BRIAN BLACKBURN
Original French Lyric by PIERRE COUR
Music by ANDRE POPP

As before

THE LOCO-MOTION

Words and Music by GERRY GOFFIN
and CAROLE KING

MacARTHUR PARK

Words and Music by
JIMMY WEBB

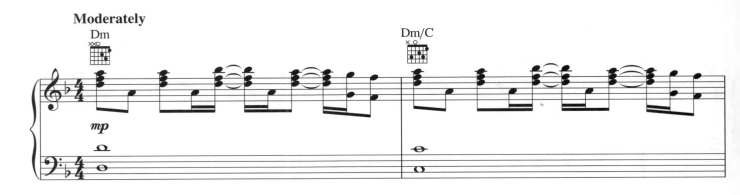

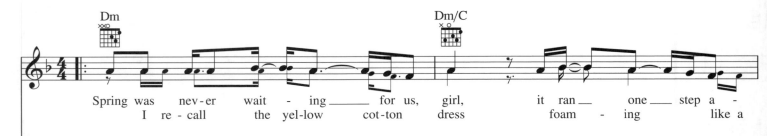

Spring was nev-er wait-ing _____ for us, girl, it ran _____ one _____ step a-
I re-call the yel-low cot-ton dress foam - ing like a

took so long to bake ___ it and I'll nev-er have ___ that rec-i-pe ___ a-

gain, oh, no. _____

MIDNIGHT CONFESSIONS

Words and Music by
LOU JOSIE

MRS. BROWN YOU'VE GOT A LOVELY DAUGHTER

Words and Music by
TREVOR PEACOCK

MY GUY

Words and Music by
WILLIAM "SMOKEY" ROBINSON

Moderately

Noth - ing you could say could tear _____ me a - way from my _____
Noth - ing you could do could make _____ me un - true to my _____

_____ guy. _____ (My guy.) _____ Noth - ing you could do 'cause I'm _____
_____ guy. _____ (My guy.) _____ Noth - ing you could buy could make _____

_____ stuck like glue to my _____ guy. _____ (My guy.) _____ I'm
_____ me tell a lie to my _____ guy. _____ (My guy.) _____ I

NEVER MY LOVE

Words and Music by DON ADDRISI
and DICK ADDRISI

1 2 3

Words and Music by LEONARD BORISOFF,
JOHN MADARA and DAVID WHITE

OUR DAY WILL COME

Words by BOB HILLIARD
Music by MORT GARSON

PEOPLE GOT TO BE FREE

Words and Music by FELIX CAVALIERE
and EDWARD BRIGATI, JR.

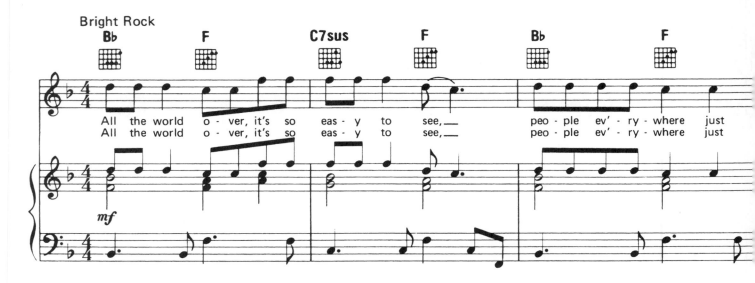

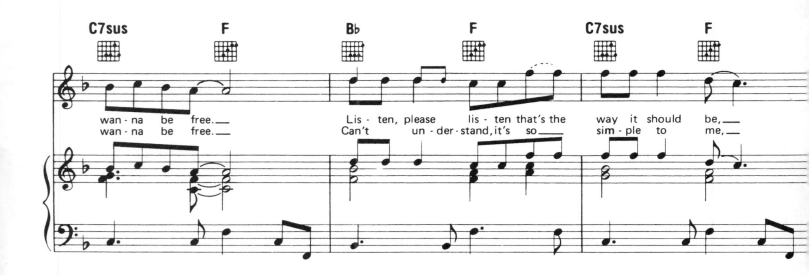

Ask me my o-pin-ion, my o-pin-ion will be,___ it's a nat-'ral sit-u-a-tion for a
Ev'-ry-bod-y's danc-in', come on let's___ go see,___ there's_ peace_ in the val-ley, now we

man to be free.____
all can be free.____

Spoken: Look, see that train over there? Now
You know it's been long now over-

that's the train of freedom, it's about to arrive any minute now.
due, Look out 'cause it's comin' right on through.

Repeat and Fade

PLEASANT VALLEY SUNDAY

Words and Music by GERRY GOFFIN
and CAROLE KING

RESPECT

Words and Music by
OTIS REDDING

PLEASE LOVE ME FOREVER

Words and Music by OLLIE BLANCHARD
and JOHNNY MALONE

PLEASE MR. POSTMAN

Words and Music by ROBERT BATEMAN,
GEORGIA DOBBINS, WILLIAM GARRETT,
FREDDIE GORMAN and BRIAN HOLLAND

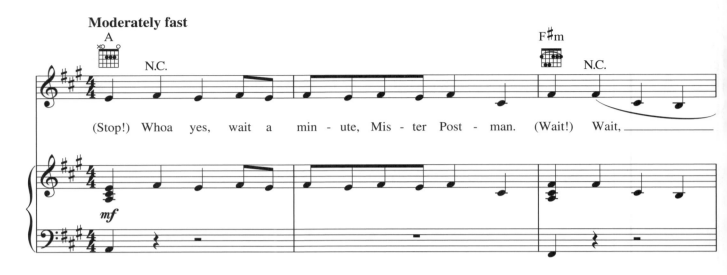

RAMBLIN' ROSE

Words and Music by NOEL SHERMAN
and JOE SHERMAN

RUBY BABY

Words and Music by JERRY LEIBER
and MIKE STOLLER

(Ru - by Ru - by Ru - by, ba - by)

(Ru - by Ru - by Ru - by, ba - by)

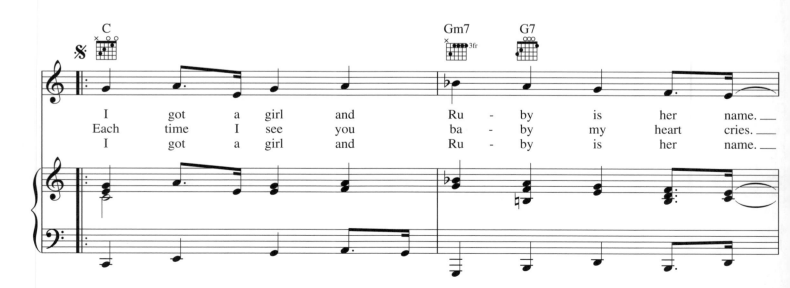

I got a girl and Ru - by is her name. ___
Each time I see you ba - by my heart cries. ___
I got a girl and Ru - by is her name. ___

SHERRY

Words and Music by
BOB GAUDIO

RUBY, DON'T TAKE YOUR LOVE TO TOWN

Words and Music by
MEL TILLIS

town. _____ For it was -n't me that start - ed that old cra - zy As - ia war, _____ but I was proud to go and do my pa - tri - ot - ic chores. _____ Oh,

SAVE THE LAST DANCE FOR ME

Words and Music by DOC POMUS
and MORT SHUMAN

Moderately, with a beat

You can dance ev-'ry dance with the one that gives you the eye; let {him}{her}
know that the mu-sic is fine, like spar-kling wine; go and

hold you tight. ___
have your fun. ___

You can smile ev-'ry
Laugh and sing, but while

smile for the one that holds your hand ___ in the pale moon-light. ___}
we're a-part ___ don't give your heart ___ to ___ an-y-one. ___}

THE SHOOP SHOOP SONG
(It's in His Kiss)

Words and Music by
RUDY CLARK

SLOOP JOHN B

Words and Music by
BRIAN WILSON

Moderately

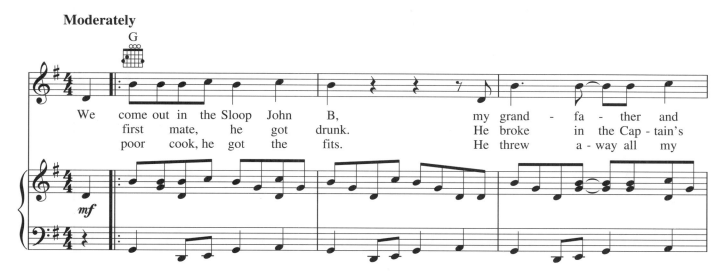

We come out in the Sloop John B, my grand-fa-ther and
first mate, he got drunk. He broke in the Cap-tain's
poor cook, he got the fits. He threw a-way all my

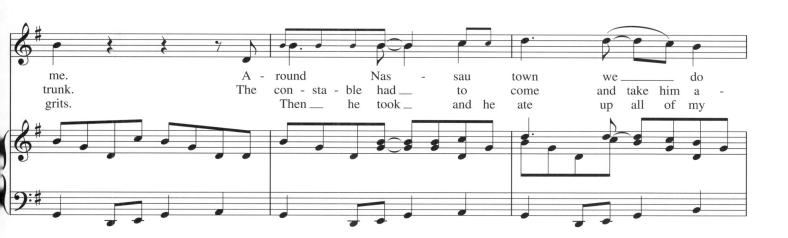

me. A-round Nas-sau town we ___ do
trunk. The con-sta-ble had ___ to come and take him a-
grits. Then ___ he took ___ and he ate up all of my

roam, drink-ing all night,
way. Sher-riff John Stone,
corn. Let ___ me go home.

SHOP AROUND

Words and Music by BERRY GORDY
and WILLIAM "SMOKEY" ROBINSON

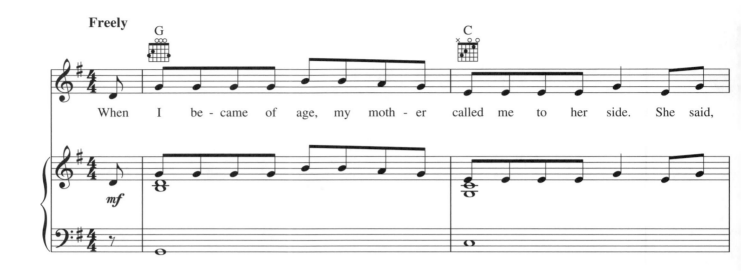

SOLDIER BOY

Words and Music by LUTHER DIXON
and FLORENCE GREEN

Medium tempo

Sol - dier boy, _____ oh, my lit - tle sol - dier boy, _____

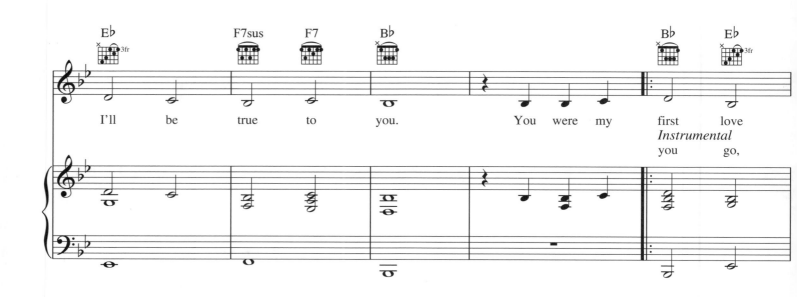

I'll be true to you. You were my first love
Instrumental
you go,

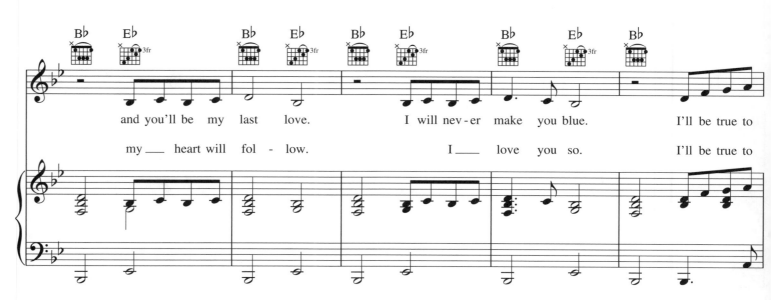

and you'll be my last love. I will nev - er make you blue. I'll be true to
my __ heart will fol - low. I __ love you so. I'll be true to

SOMETHING

Words and Music by
GEORGE HARRISON

Something in ___ the way ___ she moves, ___
Some - where in ___ her smile ___ she knows, ___
Some - thing in ___ the way ___ she knows, ___

at - tracts ___ me like ___ no oth - er lov - er.
that I ___ don't need ___ no oth - er lov - er.
and all ___ I have ___ to do is think ___ of her.

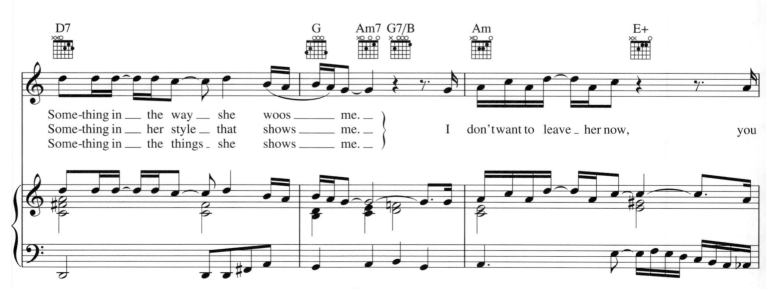

Some-thing in ___ the way ___ she woos ___ me. ___
Some-thing in ___ her style ___ that shows ___ me. ___
Some-thing in ___ the things ___ she shows ___ me. ___

I don't want to leave ___ her now, ___ you

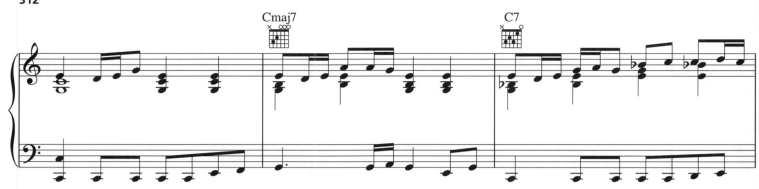

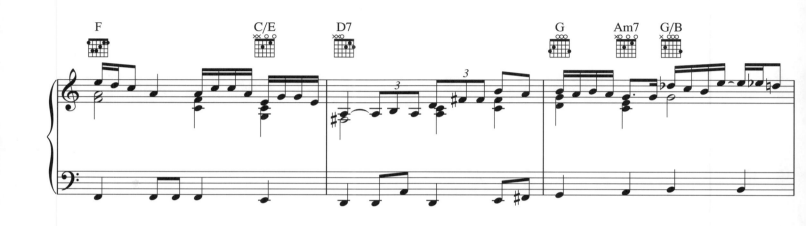

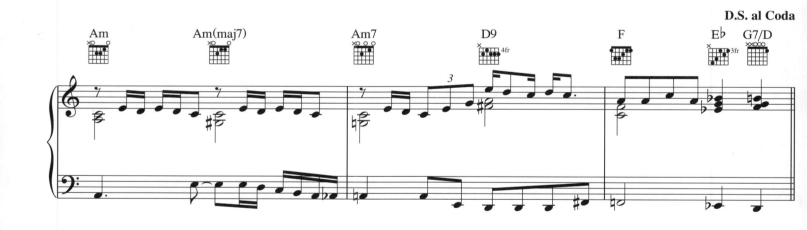

D.S. al Coda

SPOOKY

Words and Music by J.R. COBB,
BUDDY BUIE, HARRY MIDDLEBROOKS
and MIKE SHAPIRO

STAND BY ME

Words and Music by JERRY LEIBER,
MIKE STOLLER and BEN E. KING

STOP! IN THE NAME OF LOVE

Words and Music by LAMONT DOZIER,
BRIAN HOLLAND and EDWARD HOLLAND

Steadily

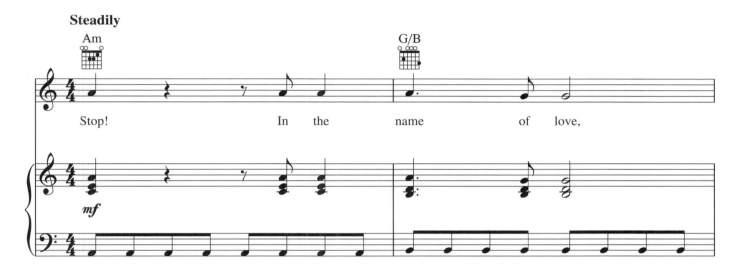

Stop! In the name of love,

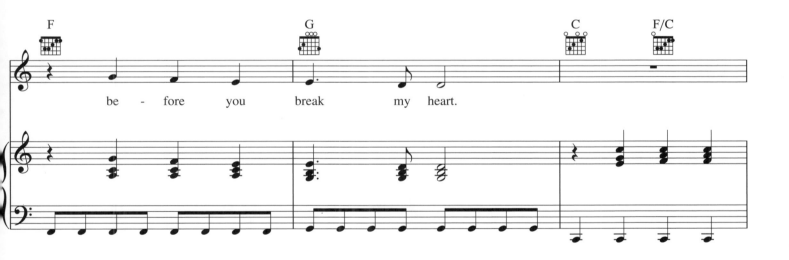

be - fore you break my heart.

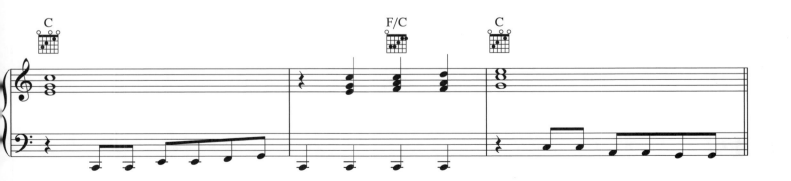

STAY

Words and Music by
MAURICE WILLIAMS

SUMMER IN THE CITY

Words and Music by JOHN SEBASTIAN,
STEVE BOONE and MARK SEBASTIAN

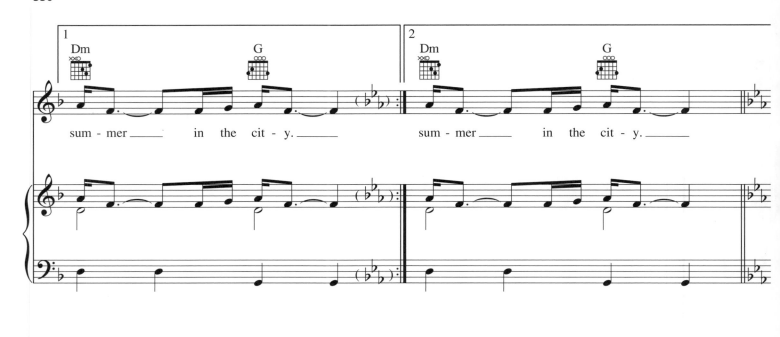

1 Dm G

sum - mer _____ in the cit - y. _____

2 Dm G

sum - mer _____ in the cit - y. _____

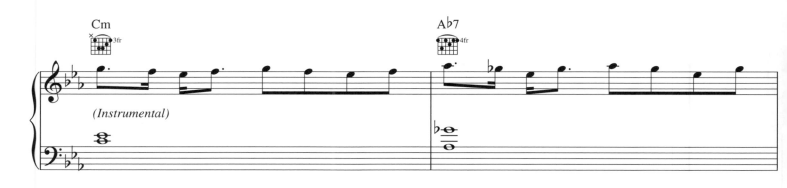

Cm   Ab7

(Instrumental)

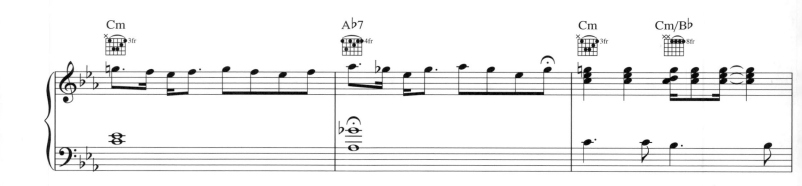

Cm   Ab7   Cm   Cm/Bb

D.S. and Fade
(Instrumental)

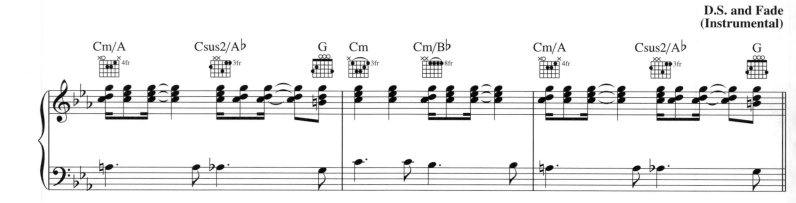

Cm/A   Csus2/Ab   G   Cm   Cm/Bb   Cm/A   Csus2/Ab   G

SURF CITY

Words and Music by BRIAN WILSON
and JAN BERRY

SUSPICIOUS MINDS

Words and Music by
FRANCIS ZAMBON

SWEET CAROLINE

Words and Music by
NEIL DIAMOND

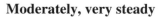

THERE'S A KIND OF HUSH
(All Over the World)

Words and Music by LES REED
and GEOFF STEPHENS

A TIME FOR US
(Love Theme)
from the Paramount Picture ROMEO AND JULIET

Words by LARRY KUSIK and EDDIE SNYDER
Music by NINO ROTA

TRACES

Words and Music by J.R. COBB
and BUDDY BUIE

TOWN WITHOUT PITY

Words and Music by DIMITRI TIOMKIN
and NED WASHINGTON

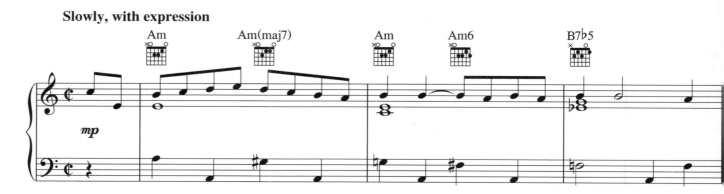

TRAVELIN' MAN

Words and Music by
JERRY FULLER

UNDER THE BOARDWALK

Words and Music by ARTIE RESNICK
and KENNY YOUNG

TWIST AND SHOUT

Words and Music by BERT RUSSELL
and PHIL MEDLEY

Moderately, with a beat

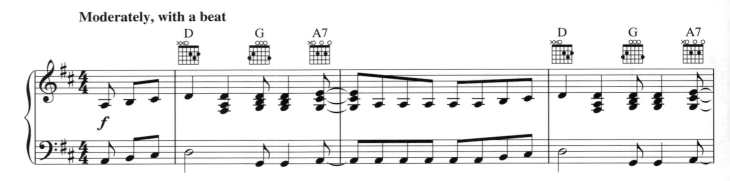

Well, shake it up ba - by, __ now,
- by, __ now, } (Shake it up ba - by) Twist and
ba - by, __ now,

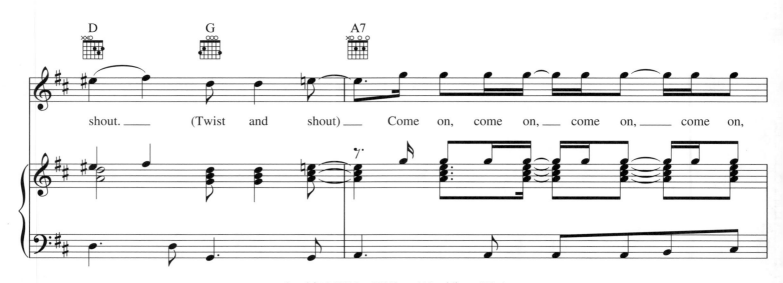

shout. __ (Twist and shout) __ Come on, come on, __ come on, __ come on,

(Like I knew you would) ___ Well, shake it up ba -
mine. (Let me know you're mine) ___

Ah

Ah

WEDDING BELL BLUES

Words and Music by
LAURA NYRO

WHERE THE BOYS ARE

Words and Music by HOWARD GREENFIELD
and NEIL SEDAKA

WILL YOU LOVE ME TOMORROW
(Will You Still Love Me Tomorrow)

Words and Music by GERRY GOFFIN
and CAROLE KING

WHITE RABBIT

Words and Music by
GRACE SLICK

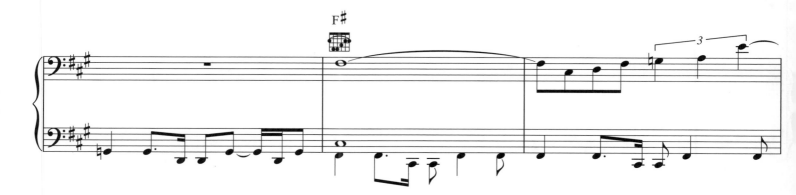

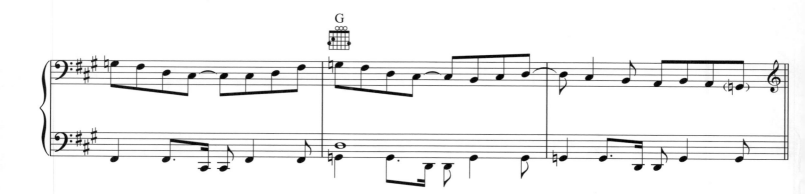

Psychedelic Stomp

WINDY

Words and Music by
RUTHANN FRIEDMAN

WORLD WITHOUT LOVE

Words and Music by JOHN LENNON
and PAUL McCARTNEY

YOU KEEP ME HANGIN' ON

Words and Music by EDWARD HOLLAND, LAMONT DOZIER and BRIAN HOLLAND

Set me free. Why don't ____ you, ba - by? (Get out my life.) (Let me be.) Why don't ____ you, ba - by? 'Cause you don't ____ real - ly love ____ me, you just keep ____

Moderately fast

Recorded a half-step lower.

YESTERDAY

Words and Music by JOHN LENNON
and PAUL McCARTNEY

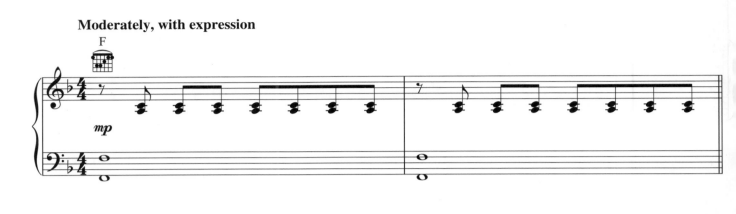

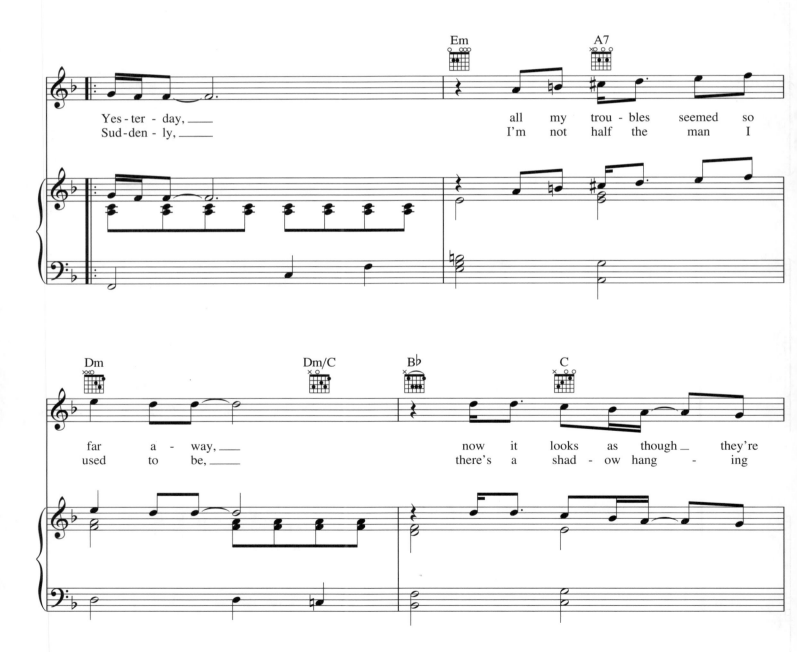

Yes-ter- day, ____ all my trou-bles seemed so
Sud-den- ly, ____ I'm not half the man I

far a- way, ____ now it looks as though ____ they're
used to be, ____ there's a shad-ow hang- ing